People like you are loving Jonny Hat

If you want to expand and explode your coaching/mentoring biz, Jonny Cooper is the man to go to.
Yayati Desai – Mind coach

Brilliant insights, lots of good tips to take away and run with!
Carmen Klammer – Founder of Totally Blissed Out

I had the jigsaw pieces... Jonny has made the picture...
Nicky O'Sullivan – Divorce Coach

I just needed the framework you helped me come up with
Bahia Maktabi – Life Coach

Quick to read, fun, thought provoking, always a great message **Jill Cowley – Pozitive Minds**

Learned heaps and now I'm ready to conquer the world
Martine Brissone – Health and Wellness Coach

Jonny's a cool guy and helps you get out of your own way!
Minnie von Mallinckrodt-Grant – TEDx speaker coach

We NEED more people like Jonny in the world. **Tonya Dawn Recla – Super Power Experts**

Supportive, encouraging, helpful! **Mike Williams – Health and Vitality Coach**

No nonsense – full of wisdom and fun! **Jo Self – Strengths Branding Specialist**

Jonny navigates you through the coaching industry's foggy waters... **Mario-Alberto Bauer – Multilingual Communications wizard**

Pure gold – never fails to deliver
Steve Blampied – The Mind Fixer

Straight-talking, genuine and a tonne of value! **Stefan Boyle – Lead generation expert**

I[...]
y[...]
M[...]

Jo[...]
idea[...] ..cian,
speak

Authe...ic, powerful and fun.
Jason Kanigan – Founder, Sales Call Overhaul

Practical, actionable insights
Nick Bottini – Performance Consultant

Jonny will help you achieve your goals **Les Latham – Motor racing career coach**

Easy to connect with, very human **Hashem Getaweh – Principal, Myles Academy**

Inspired us to think creatively!
Nicola Newland – Business manager

Full of insights and experience
Mark Sephton – International personal mentor

Great source of inspiration and practical advice! **Adam Hamadache – CEO, Direct Hotel Marketing**

Positive, infectious – a fireworks display! **David Pariera – Co-founder, Take-a-Whey**

Jonny's full of highly effective ideas **Nicole Plinston – Director, Prime Recruiting**

Genuine, inspirational and with a wealth of knowledge
Mark Hamilton-Taylor – Social Media Strategist

Jonny gets results... **Melissa Mailer-Yates – Director, Shakespuss ltd**

Tactical solutions and a strategic outlook! **Laszlo Horvath – President, Active Media**

Business strategies to improve your bottom line
Anna Geary – Property sourcing expert

JONNY HATES MARKETING

99 Ways To Get Your Ideal Clients Chasing You
Without Spending A Penny On Advertising,
Working Like A Dog Or Losing Your Mind.

Jonny Cooper

RƎTHINK PRESS

First published in Great Britain 2018 by Rethink Press (www.rethinkpress.com)

Design by Clare McCabe, www.purplestardesign.co.uk

DISCLAIMER

The contents of this book are designed to steer you in the general direction of success and away from failure, but any action you take on the basis of reading Jonny Hates Marketing is entirely your responsibility, not Jonny's, the publishers' or anyone else in the chain apart from you.

Don't even think of claiming we advised you to do anything, say anything or change anything that subsequently got you in the poo. That's you did that, not us.
Of course, if any of this stuff worked and made you any kind of fortune, large or small, that was probably down to us. In fact yes, it definitely was.

DEDICATION

For Tatsiana and Little Oscar
– *my loves, my light and my inspiration.*

ACKNOWLEDGMENTS

Mostly, thanks to YOU for reading Jonny Hates Marketing. It'd all be pretty pointless if you hadn't.

Also a shout-out to my lovely editors – Jill Cowley, Caroline King, Leila Atbi, and Hayley Bowen, my brilliant designer and publisher Clare McCabe, without whom etc etc, and to all the members of the Jonny Hates Marketing Facebook Group who motivate me to show up with my best self every day.

Finally, thanks to Marc Mawhinney for such a flattering, uplifting and faultless (!) foreword.

CONTENTS

by Marc Mawhinney

Last year, I bumped into Jonny Cooper while hanging around the same circles on social media. I was instantly intrigued by his slogan, "Jonny Hates Marketing", and wondered what that was all about.

Even though lots of people hate marketing, why would an online entrepreneur would be so open about it?!

As I got to know Jonny better, and watch what he was doing to help so many people, I became a fan of his "no fluff" approach to helping coaches, therapists, trainers and consultants get more clients. Like myself, he doesn't mince words and he lays his advice out in an easy-to-understand manner.

I was honoured when Jonny asked me to read his book and write this foreword. As I was reading it, I often found myself nodding my head in agreement while highlighting passages and scribbling notes by the sides of the pages.

At first glance the book is deceptive since it's made up of a lot of short (1 or 2 page) nuggets, but don't be fooled. This book is a goldmine for those willing to soak it all in, and - more importantly – put what Jonny talks about into action!

This is a book that you'll find yourself referencing often as you continue along your entrepreneurial journey.

Keep it close by your side and good luck...

Marc Mawhinney
"The Coach's Coach"
Founder: www.naturalborncoaches.com

INTRODUCTION

If you're a coach, therapist or trainer, you'll be aware that there are two sides to your brain.

There's the side that wants to help people, transform their lives, make a difference etc etc. That's probably performing quite well.

Then, there's the side of the brain that hates marketing.

That's the side that sucks at social media, podcasts, email campaigns, funnels, programme structure and sales calls, and produces a neuro-chemical called despair whenever you sit down to get started on that stuff.

I'd always sucked at all that too, and as a defence mechanism I got really lazy in the mid-noughties and just kinda gave up on marketing.

After building and selling an eight-figure business, I founded a coaching practice, of sorts. Actually, it was more a consultancy, where good ol' Jonny would do pretty much anything a client asked. I got dragged into HR, marketing, sales, business development, exit strategies and even agreed to go to Kuala Lumpur to broker a yacht deal!

Tanning and invigorating though that was, I knew I had to change. Being a jack-of-all-trades didn't suit me, and I wanted to find my true purpose, my super-power and my audience.

I started to study coaching icons and digital marketers like Tony Robbins, Frank Kern, Mike Dillard, Steve Chandler and others.

Soaking up all their wisdom and experience, I discovered some fundamental truths that changed everything, and would soon make finding my ideal clients so much easier.

I've distilled those truths into what I call The Three Pillars of Effortless Marketing, and I'm going to share them with you in the Prologue, next.

Before that, just a quick bit of housekeeping to set your expectations, and make sure you get as much as possible from reading what follows:

- This isn't a book with a single rambling story – it's a collection of micro-stories. So, you can dip in and out as you like.

- Many of the chapters cover mindset – getting and keeping both sides of your brain in a healthy and positive place. Don't worry if you don't find what feels like immediately actionable tips. Everything you read will have an impact on your clarity, thoughts, habits and actions at some point.

- My dearest hope is that this stuff resonates with you in some deep-down consciousness place, and illuminates a flashing sign in your retinas that says, "Yes, NOW I get it!" If that happens, let me know. I have plenty more up my sleeve and I need the green-light from you to do another book sometime soon.

Here's to your extravagant success!

PROLOGUE

Before Marketing

I was talking to a coach recently who asked me to have a look at his "marketing", so he could start to get more of his ideal clients.

As you know, Jonny Hates Marketing, so that was never going to be a task I relished.

Anyway, I found his 3 websites, 2 Facebook business pages and 2 (really!) LinkedIn profiles and summed up the problem immediately:

He wasn't ready for marketing.

As I audited his content, messaging and offers, I saw what resembled a local jumble-sale. His ideas were unclear and inconsistent, his promises unremarkable and yet unbelievable, and he'd done nothing to demonstrate why I'd want to engage him as my coach.

And he's not alone - many coaches I meet suffer from the same lack of clarity.

Here's a short list of things to do before you start marketing:

1. Decide **WHAT** one thing you bring to the world
2. Decide **WHO** needs or wants it, and
3. Work out **HOW** you're going to package and deliver it to them

And those are the THREE PILLARS OF EFFORTLESS MARKETING!

Fundamentally, nailing down your **WHAT, WHO** and **HOW** will eliminate the ball-ache, heart-ache and headache of trying to create revenue from a vague idea.

In this client's case, he's going to have to decide which of his THREE websites, TWO FB Pages and TWO LI profiles he's going to dump, so he ends up with a MAXIMUM of ONE of each for us to work with.

First, we'll create a single, consistent, compelling message about what problem he solves or benefit he brings, and run it across all his media. That's his **WHAT**.

Next, we'll work on his ideal client avatar – his **WHO**.

Finally, we'll design a signature programme or product, build it and price it. Yes, that's his **HOW**.

Then, we might just be ready to start marketing.

So, let's get on with it!

When I was a kid, I used to hang out with this boy who was, well, different.

Years later, I realised he was autistic, but then I just knew he was different, and I enjoyed the no-nonsense way he looked at things.

We'd be playing football, and he'd say, this isn't making me happy. So we'd stop.

One time he said he felt sad. I asked why and he said, I'm hungry. So we ate, and he was happy again.

We all do stuff that makes us happy, and we all do stuff that makes us sad, but we rarely plan our actions as if there were such a simple binary choice. We just do stuff anyway, based on spurious criteria, like feeling we have to, or need to.

We can even trick ourselves into thinking we need to do something, when we really, really don't.

But, know this: if we actively strive to do only those things that make us happy, we'll be more productive and successful too.

What will you do "happy" today?

DON'T SOLVE PROBLEMS!

It's easy to get addicted to a victim's story, and to the adrenaline rush when everything is wrong or in chaos, and needs sorting out.

There's a strange sort of reward – a self-satisfaction that comes from maneuvering out of an awkward situation or solving a serious problem.

How about this for an idea?

Most of your problems are self-created, so don't congratulate yourself for wheedling your way out of them.

Just don't create them in the first place.

You are, as a wise man said, the sum of the five people closest to you.

So, if you want to create an extraordinary impact, that doesn't mean hanging out with like-minded individuals, folks you gel with just because they agree with you, or those with shared interests.

It means reaching outside of your comfort network, looking upwards to bond with those who can truly challenge, guide and inspire you.

If you're the happiest person you know – find some new people.

If you're the most successful person in your community – find another community.

If you love more than your partner – you know what's next.

Your personal brand should be a reflection of who you are, what you represent and what you're passionate about.

Contribute your voice to public discussions, forums, podcasts and more to give people opportunities to connect with you and recognise your value in their lives.

Putting work into communication, writing white papers, eBooks and blogs to build an online presence will help you achieve notoriety.

Once people accept you in relation to a specific subject or area of expertise, you will be positioned as an authority and a leader in that field.

Then the magic happens – customers will come to you, saving you the heartache and grind of having to go to them.

Be irreplaceable.

Most people never climb their Everest because they only ever do things they already can do.

By age 30, you've probably established what you're going to do, where you're going to live, and who you're going to BE.

But what would happen if you stopped doing just the things you already can do, and started doing only the things you can't NOT do?

Pick ONE thing, right now, which ignites a fire deep in your belly that drives you to be crazy, extravagant and generous with your time, effort and motivation.

Do that one thing now, and I promise everything else will change.

Remember the line about the guy going into a General Store, and they wouldn't sell him anything specific?

Many coaches are like a general store where their offering is so vague, nobody even knows what to ASK for.

Your customer has a specific problem, so set out to solve it with a specific solution.

Tell me you can turn Twitter into a money-making machine.

Say you can show me how to use funnel automation like a pro.

Offer to help turn my customers into raving subscribers.

Now you got my attention.

If your marketing isn't working as well as you would like it to there may be one simple reason...It's all about you!

Ah, you say, "But I have refined the message about my business and we are very clear on how we provide a service to our clients."

And therein lies the problem.

NOBODY WANTS TO READ ABOUT YOU!

Every single piece of marketing should be about your clients, their story and their journey.

Here are 5 simple questions to ask yourself as you review your marketing:

1. Where are my prospects right now?
2. Where do they want to be?
3. What are the hurdles they will need to overcome to get there?
4. How can I help them do that?
5. How can I add trust and credibility so they will choose me to work alongside them?

Answer these questions in your marketing messages and prospects will self-select, put up their hand and say "yes, I want to work with you."

CONNECT TO LESS

Here's what Robin Sharma calls the Zero Drama Life:

Clear out the clutter and focus mono-maniacally on a few key things that are going to get you where you want to go.

Most people are connected to too much. Think of a Tibetan monk at one end of the scale, meditating in his leafy sanctuary, overwhelmed by the aromas and sounds of nature, and mindful of the power and meaning of his own existence.

At the other end, a busy executive with twenty clients, two bosses, three phones, a Skype chat, a Facebook DM, a workout schedule, a salary that almost pays his bills but not quite, and a deadline to be home by six otherwise his dinner's in the dog.

Who's happier?

I'm not advocating you aspire to either extreme. Generally, extremes of anything are bad.

I'm suggesting you connect to only those things, people and places which make you happy, productive and successful.

Here's some wisdom about launching a new project, website, software or product.

Seth Godin says: Ship it before it's ready, because it's never ready.

Carl Benz made a motor car when it was against the law to drive.

Guthenburg launched a printing press when fewer than one in twelve people across Europe knew how to read.

Stu McLaren says: you don't have to get perfect, you just have to get going.

Think MVP – the Minimum Viable Product.

Launch it now, it's probably more than ready.

People don't remember what you say. They remember how you make them feel.

How does your customer HATE feeling?

Bored
Talked at
Not listened to
Belittled
Patronised
Confused
Stupid
Inadequate
Overwhelmed

How does your customer LOVE feeling?

Excited
Inspired
Valued
Heard
Connected
Important
Smart
Led
Mentored
Improved

Ask an unconnected stranger how your proposition, your website, your emails, your STUFF makes them feel.

Then do all your work with that in mind.

Beyond the democratic freedoms of speech, expression and movement, there are others that you can choose for yourself.

- Financial Freedom: regularly creating more income than you choose to spend.
- Time Freedom: from choosing when you work, and when you don't.
- Location Freedom: from being able to work anywhere in the world you choose.

All those freedoms come as part of the package when you build your own thriving digital business. Enduring and predictable wealth, a four-hour work week and a life of travel and mobility are all on the agenda once you get your customers to pay you for value instead of time.

All that's needed is for you to decide that it's not acceptable to be struggling for one-off sales, exchanging time for money and working morning till night in the same stuffy office.

Then choose to do it all differently.

Your choices, your freedoms.

The 5 product-launch myths that are keeping you poor and stupid:

1. You must listen to everyone's opinion.

2. You need more friends/followers/"likes" first.

3. You should try to appeal to the widest possible audience.

4. It's essential to give away your best work before you ask for money.

5. You have to include all your knowledge, skills and teachings in this one feature-laden product.

The one true myth:

A simple, single-topic offer launched with passion and vigour today always beats waiting till your perfect, wrinkle-free, all-consuming creation is ready.

[Remember: it'll never be ready]

CONSUMER VS CREATOR

We are all consumers – it's effortless. It's much harder to be a creator, which is why not everyone takes the trouble.

Your importance and impact is defined by how much value you create, never by how much you consume.

Creating something so compelling, so irresistible that we all want to consume it is one of the key markers of a successful life.

Nobody remembers the consumer, but the creator's legacy lives forever.

Get started on your beautiful creation right away. Consumers around the world are waiting.

[Postscript: creating something irresistible to your ideal client usually gives you more leverage as a consumer too, if that's your thing.]

Something that's often forgotten by small businesses, and particularly by the staff of small businesses...

"I'd never spend £400 on a pair of glasses", say the optical sales staff. And so they put up resistance on behalf of the client.

They never once think that the client might love the opportunity of spending £400 on a pair of glasses.

We all spend smart money and we all spend stupid money, and most importantly we all get the choice of what to spend it on.

Just for fun, price one of your products extravagantly expensively and see who wants to buy it.

You might be surprised at how many of us are delighted with the value you're offering.

On the 6th May 1954, Roger Bannister ran a mile in 3 minutes, 59.4 seconds. A couple of blinks slower, and nobody would know his name.

Thomas Edison tested more than 3,000 designs for a viable light bulb before filing a patent in 1879 that changed the course of history. If he hadn't displayed such remarkable persistence, we might today remember Joseph Swan, Charles Brush, Henry Woodward or Matthew Evans who were working on the idea in labs around the world at the same time.

30 publishers rejected Stephen King's draft for Carrie before Doubleday advanced him $2500 and added a few pounds in weight to bookshelves everywhere.

The margins between success and failure are often so small that you can't imagine how close you are right now.

At this point, therefore, the choice to push a little bit more is yours.

You can spend your life striving for financial riches – and if that's what makes you happy, you probably should.

Consider these other elements of a great life:

- Having long meals with loved ones
- Watching amazing sunsets and full moons
- Taking walks in the woods on crisp Autumn days
- Laughing hard with new friends
- Getting big hugs from your babies
- Receiving heartfelt appreciation
- Giving genuine thanks
- Feeling passion and fulfilment
- Sleeping well and easily
- Being spectacularly fit and healthy

If you can tick more than 3 of these, you're already wealthy.

We can all visualise success and what it will feel like when we get there. Cars, houses, holidays, cash, acclaim, contentment... add your own to the list.

What's harder to visualise, and even harder to commit, is what it takes to get us there.

The success gap is the distance between what you want and what you're prepared to give to get it.

I read a great quote from the manager of a small, underfunded IndyCar racing team in the States.

This is a sport where hundreds of millions will get you to the top, and this team is working with tens. They compensate for their relative lack of budget with uncommon commitment, blood, sweat and tears.

Here's what the guy said:

"This team is not just working to survive; it is fighting to succeed."

And there's the thing: Maybe it's not just about how hard you work.

It's about how hard you fight, and why.

Distraction = Inaction, and there's no greater distraction from our mission than the connected world we're immersed in.

To break free from destructive media addictions, we need to dramatically change our habits and take back our lives so we can create, dazzle and achieve.

Here are some ideas:

1. Limit media consumption to 60 minutes a day – that includes emails, TV, YouTube and social media
2. Look at emails twice a day, and NEVER in the first or last 60 minutes of the day
3. Turn off ALL visual and audible notifications on your smartphone and PC
4. Never, EVER expose yourself to news on TV, newspapers or online. It's all designed to get you addicted and is always negative
5. Don't look at ANY screens in the last hour before bed

The internet's only working for you if you're controlling its impact on you.

You wouldn't tolerate a human standing by your shoulder talking randomly and continuously at you all day, so why allow media to do the same?

The Low Media Diet might just be the best thing you do this year.

NETWORKING FOR IDIOTS

Every chance you get to network turns out the same.

You show up in a room at least two thirds-full of strangers and you catch an eye here, a smile there.

Spotting someone who seems like your most interesting next move, you wander over, trying not to stride too eagerly towards them.

One of your three stock opening lines is right there on your lips, and idly tumbles out with a dull thud, like a sleeping baby rolling out of bed onto the floor.

- How are you?
- Where are you from?
- What do you do?

The conversation starts with a whimper, and just winds down from there.

Next-day result: A bunch more dog-eared business cards to gather dust on your desk for the next three years.

Networking 2.0: try these questions instead!

- What's the biggest thing you're working on right now?
- What do you need most in your business this year?
- How are you helping folks like me these days?

The conversation is engaging, flowing and might just lead somewhere.

Next-day result: A bunch of new connections, enthused and empowered to do great work, maybe even with you!

Come on, raise your game...

I've spent the last 3 months setting my wake-up call 5 minutes a week earlier.

I haven't made 5 am quite yet – I might never – but I've shaved an hour off my daily start-time and am in the saddle by 6.15.

Results?

- More productive – I have another 60 minutes to read, write and create each day
- More healthy – My gym visits don't seem to be eating into my workday anymore
- More power – By the time 9am comes around, I'm already invigorated and completely switched on

I'd love you to have all that for yourself, but here are some cautionary notes:

1. Don't flush your extra time away on social media. It'll crush your spirit for the rest of the day and anyway, what's the point?

2. Don't try and get up an hour early in one go. It'll feel like jet-lag. 5 minutes a week is fine – ten if you can cope.

3. Make a list of goals the night before. If getting focused in the morning is ever an issue for you, it'll be even more so the earlier you wake.

4. Write down daily what extra you've achieved with your new regime. It's important that something more has happened.

5. Don't steal the time from your sleep. Go to bed earlier to keep your body and mind at their peak.

Getting up earlier could be the greatest productivity hack of the decade.

We talk about "gaining" trust, as if it's simply a matter of persuading others that you're capable of being believed.

In reality though, there are two different types of trust:

1. Internal Trust AKA Confidence.

If you don't believe yourself and don't think you're worthy of our approval and support, why should we? Do something that makes you happy and ignites passion in you every day. Do the stuff that only YOU can do. In fact, do the stuff you can't NOT do. Soon you'll trust yourself enough to change other people's lives too.

2. External Trust AKA Credibility.

When you have earned your own trust, you'll be singing your song so loud and clear that everyone will know you're worth trusting. You don't have to work at building trust. Just do great work and put it out there so we can see it. Trust will come naturally.

Trust me.

As Seth Godin says, you might not get the microphone back for a while.

But that's no reason to blather, or demand that your audience listens to a litany of stuff you think you need them to hear.

Nothing works better than a single, clear message. Here's some examples:

- What one thing do you want me to do when I click on your website? It's called the Most Wanted Action (MWA) and I need to be able to work it out in under 3 seconds.

- Don't email colleagues with a to-do list to be worked through by tomorrow. Ask them to do one thing, now.

- When you're presenting to a live audience, stick to the topic. Deviation is a crime that leaves our heads spinning.

- Facebook ads/flyers/tweets not working? It might be because we can't read your message for padding and waffle. Cut out ten words and try it again.

- Rambling email newsletters with updates about YOU are a lousy way to stay in touch with your audience. Better to send us a quick note asking us to actually DO something specific and useful.

- We don't want to read about your wide-ranging skills and roles on your business card. If a two-word title can't tell us what you do, it's probably a made-up job anyway.

You wouldn't ask your spouse to grab you a beer, bring your slippers, change the TV channel, book the vacation and walk the dog.

You might get one of those at best (more likely none) so don't burden us with your woolly wish lists either.

The Oxford Dictionary defines fitness in two ways:

1. The condition of being physically fit and healthy
2. The quality of being suitable to fulfill a particular role or task

Let's merge the two definitions into a third:

3. The quality of being physically fit and healthy enough to fulfill a particular role or task

Right now, your "roles or tasks" are your life and your career.

Here are some life and career goals you might have:

- I want to be alive and healthy as my children grow up and have children of their own
- I want to be able to continually reinvent and improve myself
- I want to retain full mobility and stamina throughout my life

If you're physically fit, it means that your body is as capable as your mind. In fact, your body IS your mind, and your mind IS your body.

But here's the thing: **Unless you're an Olympic athlete or a personal trainer, fitness is not a goal, it's a tool**.

- You don't need "killer" abs, whatever they are.
- You don't need to run marathons.
- You don't need to bench-press 300lbs.

You simply need a level of fitness which gives you the ability to achieve your primary life and career goals.

As you build your authority as a change-maker, you will often get asked questions like:

- Can I get your opinion on x?
- Can you take a look at my new website/Facebook page/ blogpost etc?
- Can I pick your brains for a minute?

There's a middle ground between pulling out your fee-table or rolling over and doing it for nothing:

Ask them to make a small donation to charity, or send them a link to your Amazon wish-list and let them decide what they think your time is worth.

I'm not judging you either way, but they're both better options than doing it for free.

Why?

Because that which has no cost, has no value.

Plus, if you learn how to get your clients to pay for everything you do, that's the first step to finally getting paid what you're worth.

Getting stuff done while still leaving time for family and friends can be a massive challenge for entrepreneurs like us.

Here are some of my life-balancing habits:

- **Establish cut-offs** and stick to them. I share my diary with the family so they can hold me to account for spending non-work time with them
- **Let clients know** when they can interact, and when they can't. This'll foster respect and authority. What does it say about you if you're ALWAYS available?
- **Make virtual meetings** the default, to limit travelling and maximise home-time. Unless you work on a plane, bus or train there's no excuse for spending half your life in transit.
- **Work from a home-office**. Punctuate your day with food and rest breaks in the real world.
- **Learn to delegate**, automate and abdicate from doing everything possible in your business. That way you can take breaks, take vacations and it's all still there when you get back.

One thing I wish for you more than anything is that you savour every moment of your single, precious, irreplaceable life, and fill it with the joy and splendour of your loved ones.

Don't be that person who looks back and wonders where the time went, and why the kids aren't kids anymore.

Just don't.

You may have heard of the rocks analogy coined by time-management guru Steven Covey.

It's where you start with a large empty glass, a half-dozen big rocks, a bunch of smaller pebbles, and a pile of sand. The task is to fit as much into the glass as possible, and of course you get more in if you start with the large rocks, let the pebbles fill the space between them and finally top-up with the sand.

If we map the analogy to a day in the life of an entrepreneur, it probably goes something like this:

Big Rocks:

- Sleep
- Family time
- Exercise
- Food
- Business strategy
- Client meetings and service delivery
- Important proposals

Pebbles:

- Marketing
- Reading
- Answering important emails and other communications

Sand:

- Social media
- TV
- Web browsing

Try "rocking" your week, and see if you Get More Done.

It's been said that your life path is set by the choices you make before you're 30, and that if you haven't "made it" by age 40, you probably never will.

While it's true that most people's careers follow a steady and predictable route, the life of an entrepreneur or creator can twist and turn forever.

Here are some inspirational folks who never gave up trying and eventually cracked it:

- Ray Kroc launched McDonald's in his 50s
- Sam Walton founded Walmart aged 46
- Charles Darwin's masterwork on evolution was published when he turned 50
- At 62, "Colonel" Sanders franchised the first KFC
- Henry Ford was 45 when he built the Model T
- Peter Roget started work on his thesaurus at 61

Exceptional examples, perhaps, but author George Eliot had a point when she said,

"It's never too late to be what you might have been".

It takes courage, as well as vision, to change the direction of what seems like your certain future.

But you can, and probably should.

Only an eccentric millionaire would stand at the roadside handing out wads of cash, but many of us do that unthinkingly with our lives.

Money is an infinite resource. It will never run out, but your time certainly will.

We are somehow able to calibrate what constitutes a waste of money, yet we spend precious little thought on what might be wasting our time.

Next time someone asks you for a chat, respond as if they'd asked you to gift them £1,000 with no chance of getting it back.

I'm not saying you shouldn't, just that you should know what you're giving away.

As author Derek Sivers says in his book Anything You Want:

"When you make a business, you get to make a little universe where you create all the laws"

In other words, it's your game, your rules.

With that in mind, if you're not...

- Deliriously happy every day you go to work
- Continuously growing and creating financial freedom
- Impacting positively on the lives of others, all the time

... then, what the hell are you playing at?

Too many entrepreneurs fuss over pricing, when really all they need fuss about is value.

If you have what someone needs and wants, price is irrelevant.

Also, people pay different prices for the same thing in different situations:

- A bottle of wine in a restaurant costs 3 times what it costs in a supermarket

- You could have 20 cups of instant coffee at home for the price of one proper cup in a coffee shop

- You pay 10x more for an airline ticket the day before the flight compared to 6 months before

- Good advice is more expensive when you're almost sunk than when you're nicely afloat

- A divorce costs way more if only you want it, and way less if you both want it (sometimes)

Learn the art of value pricing, and you'll never go short.

More importantly, neither will your customers.

IGNORE ALMOST EVERYONE

The old cliché about "you can't please everyone" was probably coined to cover the situation where some solitary someone, somewhere, expressed displeasure at something somebody said or did.

In the new world of universal connectivity and reach, it's now a given that you won't please everyone.

In fact, you'll likely be way closer to pleasing almost no-one, and that's still OK.

With 3bn people online, you only need a tiny fraction of 1% to notice you and love what you're doing.

So, focus down like crazy, find your ravenous tribe and serve them your best work.

To hell with the rest of us.

In an age when pretty much any strategy, tactic or action is possible, you need to be measuring everything to see what actually works, and what doesn't.

Analytics, tests, surveys, studies are available to all at a click or a swipe.

Here are some rules to master the art of measuring:

1. Understand WHY you're measuring, as a guide to WHAT to measure.
2. Do enough of a thing for the measurements to be valid. Dropping a great idea because it didn't work once, screws with your brain and your business.
3. Change no more than one variable at a time before re-measuring, or you won't know what caused the changed result.
4. When something measures up well, do more of it till it measures up not-so-well.
5. Don't get emotionally attached to an idea or action. Only do what the measurements tell you is working.

Of course, the starting point has to be an inspired leap into the unproven unknown, supported by your courage to create something that's not supported by data.

Something that might work, but might not.

Something that will change the world if you're right.

You need data, but we also want to hear what your instincts are telling you, because infinite data can't give us that.

AUTOMATION AND YOU

Marketing automation is one of key pillars of a digital lifestyle, covering everything from emails sent and received, social media interactions and posting, to membership offers and content.

It's the glue that holds everything else together, but there's a stage before you should even think about automation, and it's called process.

Before you automate, you have to work out what it is you're automating.

You need to manually lay out:

- everything you do in a working day
- every offer you make to your customers,
- every action they could take in response, and
- every reaction you can take in response to those

Then, tick off which of all those things you don't have to manage personally and plan your automation.

Manual before Automatic.

I heard someone today remarking how they couldn't afford a business coach.

Let's be clear: If you have a coach or mentor who's costing you money, something's wrong.

Anyone involved with your business has to demonstrate a clear ROI – Return On Investment.

You wouldn't tolerate an employee who routinely cost you more in salary than she created in gross profit.

With that in mind, why wouldn't you want to engage a coach who'll return more than her costs in extra income?

It should be the best investment you'll ever make.

LEARNING FROM GURUS

It's good to fill your network with successful people who can inspire and motivate you.

It's also good to go out of your immediate circle and taste some wisdom and experience from the true greats.

Here are some of my favourite musings from people who've earned the right to be called gurus:

- If you can dream it, you can do it. **Walt Disney**
- The secret of getting ahead is getting started. **Mark Twain**
- Optimism leads to achievement. Nothing can be done without hope and confidence. **Helen Keller**
- The most certain way to succeed is to try just one more time. **Thomas A. Edison**
- When something is important enough, you do it even if the odds are not in your favour. **Elon Musk**
- If you want to conquer fear, don't sit home and think about it. Go out and get busy. **Dale Carnegie**
- Be kind whenever possible. It is always possible. **Dalai Lama**
- Things do not happen. Things are made to happen. **JFK**

In summary: self-belief, action, tenacity, purpose and kindness.

Five habits that, taken together, almost guarantee success.

PASSION, PURPOSE, PROFITS

Over the last couple of decades, I've been lucky enough to be involved with over 100 businesses run by clients, partners and well, just me.

When I look back and examine the failures and the successes, a clear pattern emerges:

- Those businesses we started just to make us money and create financial freedom did neither, and eventually failed.

- When we created something because we were passionate about the cause, and would happily have done it for free, it worked out well each time.

If we thought something would make us rich, we were basing that on evidence from other people. We were transfixed with their success, not the potential for ours.

Or we said, "that industry's booming right now, so let's get on the gravy train".

Guess what? Whenever we jumped on a gravy train, the gravy turned cold and lumpy, and we couldn't wait to pour it down the sink.

If you work at an idea only because you think it's going to make you rich, you'll always under-perform, and you'll always be looking for a way out.

That doesn't mean you shouldn't pursue profit – in fact you absolutely should, and like crazy – but you have to start with something that lights a raging fire inside you.

Be happy. Be fulfilled. Get rich.

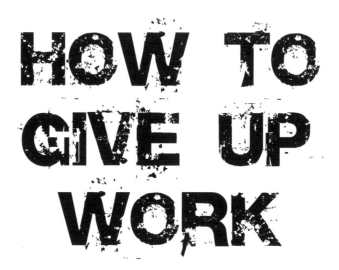

Whenever I've set up a business, I've always aimed to make myself redundant by year three at the latest.

I don't mean literally out-of-work, I mean redundant from everyday, repetitive tasks, by building a team to do the heavy-lifting that doesn't excite me or need me.

The great thing about starting your own digital business as a coach, trainer or therapist is that most of the essential processes are completely automatable, either by human resource or by digital tools.

When you've got teams and systems running your social media, your graphic design, your website, your email campaigns and customer service, that'll leave you free to simply create compelling products and solutions to dazzle and amaze your raving fans.

Now, that doesn't sound like work at all, does it?

Sales guru Art Sobczak tells how he coached a CEO to do an experiment with one of his new sales guys.

The CEO had to tell the rookie that the only people who would listen to his pitch were the execs at the very TOP level of the prospect companies.

The rookie was then told that the only deals he was allowed to sell were BIG deals.

Within a month, the new guy was outselling ALL the other sales team. And not by a bit, but by orders of magnitude.

Why?

The new boy had no idea he should go slugging it out with middle-management, and it certainly never crossed his mind to be peddling the small stuff.

Seven Lessons:

1. All that limits us is ourselves.
2. Thinking BIG gets BIG results
3. It takes just as much energy to ask for a small deal as it does to ask for a big one
4. When you expect big deals, that thought becomes a part of every action you take
5. If you miss out on a big deal, you might pick up a smaller one anyway. This doesn't work the other way round
6. Who you target in an organisation dictates the size of the deal
7. The higher you target, the more likely you'll find quick thinking decision-makers to say yes, NOW

Ask for BIG, and you might get it. Ask for SMALL and that's the most you'll EVER get.

Question: Are your products/services big enough, and are you asking the right people to buy them?

I was reading an interview with veteran American songwriter and artist Neil Young, where he said:

"What I do next is as important as anything I've ever done. More important, in fact."

That's a common theme amongst the great achievers. They often have little respect for what they did yesterday, or the day before.

Enzo Ferrari routinely ordered the destruction of last season's Formula One machines.

His favourite racecar was the next one he built.

The BBC systematically erased tapes of legendary broadcasts to make space for new recordings.

Sitting on laurels is not a success trait.

What are you going to do next?

I recently spent an inspiring afternoon with the owners of the remarkable MoBro's, the UK gentlemen's beard grooming business that's about to go vertical.

Here are some of the elements that are driving the success of this brilliant venture:

- The close-knit founder-team of 3 brothers who share identical goals and pursue them with passion and vigour
- Fabulous products serving a very focused niche, perfect for recurring subscriptions
- A mischievous sense of fun in the company's DNA
- Rabid desire to outsource everything except that which only THEY can do
- Profitable and thriving after less than three years from launch

Benchmark your venture against that list and ask – how many of those describe your business today?

9 School Habits Your Business Should Adopt

1: Curriculum – Your written business plan, containing specific, measurable and time-sensitive goals.

2: Timetable – The only way a school or business can function is by scheduling and organising days, weeks and months into manageable chunks of productivity.

3: Exams – Test your business progress regularly against your goals. Did you sell enough? Did you meet cash-flow and profitability projections? Equally, are there literally courses you or your team should be taking to improve your knowledge?

4: Terms – Punctuate your business year into easily measurable units. There is nothing like an end-of month target to keep your sales mojo fired up.

5: Awards – Recognise personal as well as personnel achievements. Bonuses, promotion and team-building events can reap far more than they cost.

6: Hierarchy – Appointing managers with the right combination of experience, knowledge, wisdom and gravitas will ensure a happy and productive classroom. Sorry, workforce.

7: Playtime – No-one functions effectively after more than an hour sitting at a computer screen. Take a 5-minute break walking, talking, or meditating.

8: Eat! – Lunch is not for wimps; it's essential. Your afternoons will be only half as useful as your mornings if you're hungry.

9: Learn and teach – Nobody knows everything, or nothing. Freely offer your knowledge to others, and listen to them in return.

The most important things in life have nothing to do with "things".

In my life, the things I focus on can't be bought:

- Building meaningful relationships with my audience
- Creating impact through helping people
- Spending quality time with my family
- Practising my daily movement routine
- Improving at least something I do every day

Strangely, as I do more of those things, I have more financial resource to buy "things", assuming I want to.

How are your *things* looking?

I hear entrepreneurs frequently saying how they ran out of something or other.

If only they had more of xxxx they'd be OK.

Here's the truth:

- You didn't run out of time. You just chose to spend it on something else.
- You're never out of options. You just haven't thought of the one you need yet.
- You haven't run out of ideas. They're all in your head, waiting for the reason to emerge.
- You're not out of breath. You're training your lungs to work better.
- You're not out of your comfort zone. It's growing all the time to accommodate your behaviour.
- You don't run out of luck. Practise harder, and make some more.
- You're not out of money. It's just elsewhere, waiting for you to deserve it.

There's an endless supply of most things.

You just have to be ready to find it.

I was reading a former colleague of Elon Musk describing how the Tesla/Space-X billionaire is so good at getting things done quickly that he even "pees fast".

I remember sharing an office with an inspirational entrepreneur who launched over a dozen businesses in the two years I knew him. He always RAN up and down the 3 flights of steps to reach his office from the ground floor.

Both those stories describe not only the mindset of success, but they also point to the culture of urgent action that great leaders are able to inspire in their ventures.

Getting things DONE, and now, is one of the most important abilities you need to develop.

The opposite: procrastination, delay, postponement, indecisiveness, self-doubt – none of these things will help you create the life of your dreams.

So there you have it. Pee quickly and run up the stairs.

As my Dad used to say, there's an easy way and a hard way to do most things.

Here are some examples I come across every day in business:

EASY WAY: Engage in conversations with people
HARD WAY: Start selling to everyone as soon as you meet them

EASY WAY: Ask people about themselves
HARD WAY: Tell people about you

EASY WAY: Speak quietly, clearly and with a big message
HARD WAY: Strut around like a boss and shout a lot

EASY WAY: Adapt your services to your clients' needs
HARD WAY: Push people round to your way of thinking

EASY WAY: Hold the saw lightly and let the blade do the work
HARD WAY: Force the saw through the wood with all your strength*

*My Dad most often brought up the Easy/Hard adage when I was attempting "woodworking" – AKA breaking saw blades.

Not sure if there's a business analogy there, but it sure rings true with sawing.

Some questions:

- Why are some people massively successful while others struggle to make a living?
- How can one person amass a personal fortune doing what thousands of others do to almost no effect?
- How can so few of us actually breakthrough and manage what the rest only dream of?

How can **you** achieve that? How can **you** become the 1%?

One of the key drivers of ultimate success, if not THE key driver, is the strength of your network.

Connections.

You'll become the 1% by connecting to people who can help you get where you want to go.

Sadly, 99% of people are disconnected. They haven't worked out who they need in their success network, and who to keep out.

Even if they've identified worthwhile goals for themselves, they allow themselves to be influenced by others who disconnect them from those goals, sometimes forever.

I don't want this to be YOU. You don't have to live a disconnected life.

Do a connection audit today – how many of your network are inspirational mentors, coaches, supporters, and partners? How many are dead-weight, or worse?

Your network is your net-worth.

I heard a chap in a bar the other night saying "it takes money to make money" to his mate as they discussed the automatic success of some lucky rich guy they both knew.

Here's some actual truisms about why businesses succeed:

- They have a great idea
- They execute the idea with passion and commitment

The excuse of not having enough money is rarely true, and even then it's only ever partially responsible for a business failure.

In fact, having too much money can be just as catastrophic.

I've bootstrapped 7 ventures, including one which grew to a £10m turnover from zero without a penny of cash beyond revenue from sales.

If "not having money" is stopping you building the business and the life of your dreams, maybe it's time to find another business.

COINCIDENCE? NAH.

So here's what happened.

In a ten-minute break today, I take a favourite book down from my overstocked shelf and start thumbing through it.

An hour later, I'm on an impromptu video call with a guy who happens to be attending the same course as me this weekend.

I idly mention the book I'd chosen earlier, and he says yeah, I love that too.

It's pretty obscure, to say the least, and I've never met anyone else who read it, let alone liked it.

We're both musicians.

Turns out we also have similar views on coaching, and are probably at a comparable stage in terms of our reach and impact.

Next, I learn we both have Russian wives. Well, I already knew I did, but you get my drift.

None of which happened by chance or coincidence. In fact, these things rarely happen without a purposeful desire to make new connections, to listen and to learn.

I was reminded of the immortal quote from Charles "Tremendous" Jones:

"You will be the same person in five years as you are today except for the people you meet and the books you read."

Don't stay the same.

Meet people. Read. Grow.

FINDING YOUR NEXT CUSTOMER

When I surveyed start-ups and entrepreneurs in my network recently, I asked them what was the one thing that was holding them back.

After "lack of money" (which is probably just a misunderstanding anyway) the number two most popular answer was "not having enough customers".

Marketing.

Here's a thought: What if calling it "marketing" and scaring yourself with the enormous scope of that word is paralysing a simple, clear action?

If we renamed it **"finding your next customer"**?

Does that sound easier?

Over a beer last weekend, I asked a friend of mine if he knew anyone who might have a need for some brilliant recruitment software a client of mine has created.

Turns out his brother's a senior manager in one of the UK's biggest staff agencies, and within two days we have a trial underway.

I carry the message for my clients' businesses – and my own – to most every interaction I have with anyone.

Only a gentle mention, of course, not a gnarly sales pitch.

Until you've told everyone in your network about your great idea, don't even think about marketing to people you don't know yet.

That just sounds too hard to me.

Allowing other people and situations to control your thoughts and feelings is one of the easiest habits to fall into, and also one of the most debilitating to your success.

Of course, that whole sentence is a simple misunderstanding, as it's not them, it's YOU that's making you think and feel how you do.

In fact, you're the only person who can ever make you think or feel anything at all.

Here's some thorny issues that might resonate:

- You leave home after an argument with your spouse and feel angry all day

- The business partner who ripped you off ten years ago has made you wary, distrustful and incapable of forming other fruitful relationships

- Your neighbour's obvious and public success – new cars, holidays, home improvements – makes you feel inadequate and a failure

- You get an unexpected bill so you worry for a week about how you're going to manage

- The news reports on the future economic climate have convinced you that it won't be your fault if you fail to make your fortune

In each case, it might seem like your thoughts and feelings are the inevitable result of the external circumstances.

But they're not, truly they're not.

Just decide what you want to think, how you want to feel, and you will.

Scanning through a sales manual I wrote 20 years ago (I know, I'm old) I came across a section on avoiding objections.

Notice it's not about **overcoming** objections, as that's pretty hard. Avoiding them in the first place is waaay easier, and more fun.

Here's what I wrote:

Why Objections Occur, and some Objection Avoidance Techniques (OATs) by a young(er) Jonny Cooper:

- The client has misunderstood something you have said.
  OAT - Check for their understanding whenever you answer a question or make an important statement.
- You have not acted on the client's problems and needs.
  OAT - Ask for their goals at the start of the meeting, check again during, and confirm at the end. Then work towards solving them.
- You have misunderstood something the client has said.
  OAT - Ask for conformation of important statements the client makes – "just so I understand your needs, what you are saying is...."
- The client wasn't expecting you to ask him to buy anything.
  OAT - Use a trial close early on in the meeting or call – "If I can put together something to meet your needs, is there any reason we can't be getting it set up today?"
- The client doesn't like/trust you.
  OAT - Build rapport and then ensure that the client is prepared to deal with you – "Are you happy for me to work with you on this?"
- The client wants to ask someone else's opinion.
  OAT - At the first meeting, ask "Is there anyone else you need to consult before we can get started?

Good, ethical sales techniques are evergreen, aren't they?

I'm lazy. There, I've said it.

I hate using 400 words when 132 will do (count up this chapter).

I also hate marketing, the hard way anyway.

So when I'm working with a client or customer, I look for the shortest, easiest route to the next one.

And this is it:

Intelligent referrals.

Here are some examples:

You're a massage therapist. Ask your client, who's the one person you know who's always in pain from sport?

You're a financial adviser. Ask your client, who's the wealthiest person you know?

You're a mind coach. Ask your client, who's the wealthiest, most screwed-up person you know? (Then smile...)

FYI – We're running that last approach with a mindfulness coach who's getting wonderful traction with it right now.

What's your lazy, intelligent referral question?

I wrote a Facebook post recently, which polarised my audience.

Not only that, but it seemed to attract more comments and reactions than anything I've posted in a while.

What I'd done, without really thinking of the consequences, was expressed my opinion on a topical subject.

I nailed my colours to the mast and let the world know where I stood.

In response, the world told me which half agreed with me, and which half didn't.

In the future, I can direct stuff at the former, knowing at the very least that they're listening and open to my ideas.

Finding out who's in your tribe and who never will be is pretty useful data, I reckon.

THE POWER OF CONVERSATION

Like many of you, doubtless, I've subscribed to these self-styled gurus, claiming their course will "guarantee you a 7-figure launch", whatever that means.

Or maybe they'll show you how to crack the code of Facebook ads and make $50,000 a month.

But here's the news: even if any of that stuff worked – and it sometimes might – it's still a damn sight harder than putting on your game face and just talking to people.

Whatever you're selling, relationships give you opportunities that lead generation simply can't, and never will.

Every day, make 5 new LinkedIn connections, or additions to your Facebook Group.

Go to one real, live networking opportunity every week.

Then all you have to do is ask questions, listen and learn how you can serve.

Here's an idea for relationship marketing that works in pretty much any sector, with any kind of product:

Instead of finding your own ideal clients, partner with someone who already sells to your ideal clients, and share the spoils of putting your stuff out alongside theirs

For example:

- If you're a web designer, link up with a PR agency, software developer or even an office supplier to co-market and promote your offering
- If you're a massage therapist, work with a gym or a personal trainer who'll upsell your services as an add-on to their own
- If you're a business coach, find a life coach and develop complementary solutions to support the same clients
- If you're selling physical products, look for opportunities to bundle them with other similar but non-competing products

In short, one conversation to fuel hundreds or even thousands of outcomes.

You might even keep the need for lead generation at bay forever, and that's the essence of Effortless Marketing.

I was talking to a successful life coach today and he huffed about how he was in a wrangle with a client who wanted a refund.

They each had a different view of what was owed for what had been transacted, and each had converted those views into entrenched positions.

Here's my take on fees, value and refunds:

1. If a client comes on board, it's because they view the prospect of working with you as a value proposition.

2. Well done for positioning that and selling it.

3. If a client later feels they're not getting that value, it's either because you're doing a poor job, or because the client wasn't suitable for your service in the first place.

4. Either way, it's your responsibility.

5. You just learnt a great lesson which will enable you to tweak your approach for the future.

6. Refund them, with pleasure, and thank them for the experience.

7. This should be rule one: never, ever sue a client. If they dislike you enough to ask for a refund, imagine how they'll hate you after 6 weeks of litigation.

We only ever want to work with people who want to work with **us**, right?

Voluntarily, not because we forced them to.

AUTOMATE

+

DELEGATE

=

GREAT

Some of the clearest air and highest ground is reached when you are only doing what only YOU can do.

If your business depends on personal relationships (HINT: It does) then build some every day.

If you are a coach, you should coach.

If you're a designer, design stuff.

Therapists, go therapise.

What's not so smart (or even necessary) beyond establishing a process and (maybe) supervising it, is pushing paper, submitting returns, "sending" emails, managing social media and a million other seemingly worthy but incredibly expensive pursuits.

Here I mean "expensive" in the ultimate sense of the incalculable price of the time lost to your single, precious, irreplaceable life.

You are uniquely privileged to be born into an age where pretty much every mundane task is automatable, and those which aren't can usually be delegated to others way more capable and less costly than you.

Don't squander that gift by acting as if you're a Victorian shopkeeper, doing everything for yourself, by yourself.

Instead, work out what needs doing to support your mission and find who or what can do it more efficiently than you can.

We want to see your creations, not your administrations.

I read a great piece on the Entrepreneur website recently talking about why some of the best talents undervalue themselves. This manifests in them asking for too low a salary or charging fees a fraction of what they could.

The reasons for this strange behaviour are many, and include:

- Not realising how much they know, and how valuable it is to the rest of us

- Comparing themselves to others, whilst ignoring their completely different talents and journeys

- Ignoring positive feedback and focusing only on the naysayers

- Believing they've got to prove themselves further before charging or earning top dollar

- Nervous about "blowing the deal" by pricing themselves out of the market

If you're reading this, I know you're talented, ambitious, grounded and worth every penny.

Don't let the evil monkey tell you otherwise.

FACE FACEBOOK FEARS

Right now, there's no online platform better than Facebook to leverage your skills, talents and messages.

If you're in business, a reluctance to expose your authentic self to a potential audience of 2 billion is pretty much commercial suicide.

Locking down privacy, running a Secret Group or making people jump through hoops to gain permission to engage is a bit like renting a shop in the busiest-of-busy high streets, filling it with beautiful things, and then blacking out the windows.

And locking the door so we have to ring the bell to get in.

Let me explain further, with two different approaches to commonly-held views about the world's most social network:

Facebook spies on me!
A – That creeps me out
B – That means it can more easily connect me with people and stuff that might be useful

Facebook makes money from selling my data
A – That's not fair or moral
B – That means it can afford to keep all the great networking functions completely free

Everybody's on Facebook
A – It's really hard to stand out
B – When you do stand out, everybody's listening

I could run the same logic on a dozen-or-so FB whines I've heard recently.

Fact is, you're either an A-Leaver or a B-Lever.

See what I did there?

Amazon chief Jeff Bezos reports how he typically starts meetings with all participants reading the agenda and relevant memos to themselves, in silence around the table.

This focuses them on the discussions ahead, and enables everyone to begin with the same level of information received and understood.

When the session kicks off, they're all fully engaged and able to contribute effectively, creating real progress and outcomes for themselves and the business.

This is also something to try in micro-meetings and coaching calls with as few as two people involved.

Quietly absorbing a written plan for what's going to take place, along with the primary goals for the interaction, sounds like a great idea.

Anything that avoids the risk of a result-free meeting is worth a try, right?

I've met a lot of people who describe themselves as "professional" coaches, "accredited" coaches, "qualified" coaches or similar.

Now it's clear that some knowledge and authority in a coaching niche is desirable, even essential, but there's nothing to stop anyone starting out and simply helping others on their journey.

You might feel like you're not qualified, or you'd like to wait until you have "more experience"

But the truth is, NONE of that is stopping you being a great coach.

Just as the fastest way to learn something is to teach it, coaching will actually help you learn how to handle the key areas of your own life... relationships, money, health, etc.

So not only will you be helping others live their best lives, you'll also build confidence and stability in your own.

Give it a try – coach someone today!

How good are your sleep habits?

Although our lives are probably more fast-paced than those of any generation before us, we're still carrying around those same bronze-age bodies, built for 8 hours quality sleep each night.

That means keeping to the same sleep/wake routine, even at weekends, and avoiding a late night followed by a much awaited lie-in, which can impact on our ability to function at our best.

As the 2017 Nobel Prize winners discovered, short term body clock disruption affects memory formation, and in the long term it increases the risk of diseases, including type 2 diabetes, cancer and heart disease.

Here are five tips for sleeping your way to the top:

- Rise as early as you can, based on your earliest practical bedtime giving you 8 hours asleep
- Don't drink alcohol within 4 hours of going to bed
- Drink water before sleep, and as soon as you wake up
- Don't use screens – mobiles or computers – within 2 hours of bed
- Keep your bedroom as dark and cool as possible. Excess light and heat will upset your sleep rhythms

The scientists also pointed out that heart-attack risk is at its peak first thing in the morning as the body fires up the engine again for the new day.

Leaping out of bed and flinging open the curtains might not be the great idea you imagined after all...

When we're short of time – which we always are – and need to do things as efficiently as possible – which we always do – then the concept of a minimum effective dose, or MED, comes into play.

Let me explain with some examples.

- You want to meditate for 20 minutes a day? Start at 5 minutes, or 3 days a week. It will still have some effect.

- You're desperate to achieve and maintain "inbox zero"? Keep it under 20 emails and you'll feel a whole lot better.

- Your ideal is to not work Fridays, ever? Finish at midday next Friday, and every week until you're fully ready. The impact will be noticeable.

- Aiming for five new clients a month, every month? Settle at one or two for now. Your bank will see the difference immediately.

- You'd like to join the much-vaunted 5am Club? Get up at 6 every day next week. You'll get loads more done!

Think about something you want to achieve, and plot a viable intermediate stage which will get you ready for the bigger ultimate change.

It's like "baby steps" for grown ups.

I'm not one for reinventing the wheel. I'd rather slap a sticky new tyre on it and maximise traction with the least effort.

When it comes to getting more clients, here are three perennially great ideas which will never go flat:

1. **Focus on solving ONE problem for them.** You already know what's bugging your clients – if you don't, you should – so go out in the world with your ONE solution.

2. **Contact former clients.** Who's more likely than people who've used your products and services before to do so again? If you haven't spoken to your old flames in a while, do it right away.

3. **Focus on making ONE sale.** It's not a phone session, a marketing campaign, or even a newsletter. It's a quest to find the NEXT customer. When you've figured that out, do it again, and again.

Sometimes, the old ways are the best.

When you're selling a product or service that needs a "presentation" or a "proposal", it's very easy to get caught up in the mechanics of the process – the Powerpoint, the PDFs, the laptop and cables – and forget the only important part: **making the bloody sale.**

If you were to reverse-engineer a successful sale, here's what it would look like, most of the time:

- You started off by confirming that the person you were dealing with had the sole capacity and **authority** to make the buying decision

- You then asked them if and why they needed whatever it was you were trying to sell them, and why **now**

- You didn't forget to ascertain that their financial **means** were aligned with the cost of your offering

- You used **trial closes** throughout – eg – "If I can solve those problems within your budget, is there any reason we can't be getting this set up straightaway?"

- You got as much commitment as possible on the first call or meeting, even asking them to buy right there and then

- You avoided mailing out lengthy follow-ups or proposals (they never read them) and instead arranged a second face-to-face meeting to bring the deal home

And guess what happened next? They bought!

THE PAPERCLIP STRATEGY

Ever heard of Trent Dyrsmid?

He's passed into business folklore as the guy who committed to 120 phone calls a day as a rookie stockbroker, keeping track of them by moving one of 120 paperclips from one jar to another for each call he made.

When one jar was empty and the other one full, he knew he'd made 120 calls.

As he explained, "I would start calling at 8 a.m. every day. I never looked at stock quotes or analyst research. I also never read the newspaper for the entire time. If the news was really important, it would find me from other ways."

The paperclip strategy is a visual trigger, which is more powerful than another other form of productivity tool when it comes to reminding us of the importance of habit, process and consistency in our business lives.

You can use it to count how many sales emails you send, how many glasses of water you drink, or how many times you say thanks for your family and your life.

What essential habit could you measure with paperclips?

TYPES OF SPENDING

Here's a timeless, time-full truism:

Rich people spend money to save time. Poor people spend time to save money.

It's also a gross simplification, like all great truisms. But the principles behind it are fundamental to an understanding of life; namely:

1. Time is a finite resource

2. Money is an infinite resource

Read those two lines out loud, then sit quietly and just breathe.

Now answer this:

Which should you consider more, before spending loads of it?

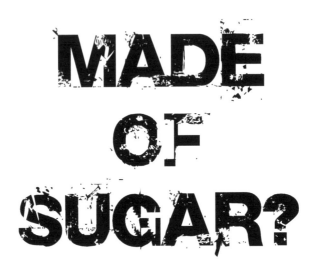

My friend Dave is a tough and rugged outdoorsman. In another time, he could have been a gold prospector in the Old West.

I once said to him that I didn't fancy going out, as it was raining. He said, but you're not made of sugar.

So, today I went for a long walk in a blustery, wet English morning, and Dave was right: I didn't dissolve.

It's easy to set the comfort bar way too low when you decide what you can and can't do.

- Have you ever turned down work because it might just be too hard?

- Do you never ask for feedback in case it's negative?

- Is there an irrational phobia stopping you doing something other people are enjoying?

- Are you worried about changing your business in case you break it?

- How about trying to improve a relationship by having an awkward conversation?

Fact is, things rarely turn out as badly as the voice in your head tells you they could.

And most times, all that dissolves is your former misunderstanding.

No, not the 70s band KISS.

I mean the 80's favourite business acronym: Keep It Simple Stupid!

It was actually a design principle noted by the US Navy in 1960, yet it's more relevant than ever in these days of infinite possibilities, exponential opportunities and ever-more-complex online tools.

If you're trying to attract clients with a service, coaching or advice designed to change their world, you can only do that with simplicity and clarity in every way.

- Ask them to tell you the ONE thing that's holding them back, right now
- Get them prepared to believe you can solve it
- Solve it
- Ask them to tell you the next thing that's holding them back
- etc etc

We don't believe you can do everything at once, and no amount of marketing you do will convince us.

In the 21st century, there's very little need for any of us to be scared.

It's very unlikely that we'll be eaten by a predator, consumed by disease or have a spell dropped on us.

Why then, do many people still seem to live their lives in a perpetual state of fear?

- Fear of trying something new
- Fear of talking to strangers
- Fear of setting audacious financial goals
- Fear of asking for a sale
- Fear of being exposed as inadequate

Fear is a redundant evolutionary hangover from the days when our lives literally hung in the balance every day.

Then, fighting or running away was a necessary tactic for survival beyond the present moment.

But now?

Fear's a distraction, generated purely by thought, by our ability to construct an imaginary future that doesn't exist yet, and most likely never will.

Get over yourself.

Fearless is the default position.

I was talking to a newbie coach last week, who explained his plans for his first 12 months in business.

He is going to build his tribe of devoted followers paying $25 a month for the most awesome collection of tutorials, eBooks and videos known to man.

All he needs is 200 subscribers and he'll be able to take it easy for a while.

Then, some of those subscribers will join his face-to-face coaching programmes and he'll live a happy and fulfilled life, he says.

Here's why doing it the OTHER way round is a much better idea:

- Getting 200 subscribers to ANYTHING is hard. Really, really hard. Especially when you don't have a ready-made audience

- Getting ONE client to agree to a face-to-face coaching programme is much, much easier

- Getting the next ten face-to-face clients gets progressively easier still as the power of referrals, recommendations and testimonials kicks in

- Working with clients 1-2-1 for a while teaches you what you need to put in an online course or subscription package later

- You'll generate case studies which you can use to eventually market your online course

- You'll create some revenue to spend on advertising. You'll NEED to advertise to get 200 subscribers.

UPDATE: Since our conversation, my newbie-coach client has taken on TWO 1-2-1 clients of his own at $500 pm each.

You have to believe that's easier than signing up 40 new subscribers!

My friend and copywriter Brian Halpin compiled a list of why your clients didn't buy from you yet:

1. You never asked
2. You never showed them how to buy
3. They don't want what you have
4. They bought from your competitor
5. They don't feel you understand them
6. They don't know, like or trust you
7. They don't believe in you enough
8. They don't believe in themselves

I'd add another one, which is actually the least important or likely, but the one you might believe to be the MOST real:

9. You're too expensive

That's almost never the case. If it was, nobody would buy a Mercedes, an iPhone or a business-class plane ticket.

Once you've ticked off Brian's 8, Jonny's number 9 is irrelevant.

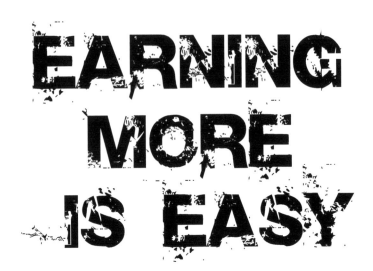

If you're a consultant, trainer, coach or therapist, there's one way above any other that'll guarantee you earn more money:

Find clients who earn more money.

As I grew a business in finance at the start of the century, I had 200 staff working for me, mostly on commission-only, and I noticed a trend.

Those who chose to work with school teachers earned a school teacher's salary in return, whereas those who decided to advise wealthy folks became much wealthier themselves.

In fact, our highest earner banked £600,000 commission in his final year with my company, after he'd set a minimum net-worth of £1m for anyone who wanted his advice.

He'd regularly fly to Dubai to meet his expat clients, who doted on him and hung on his every word.

Just by shifting his focus to a different demographic, he earned over 25x what our average adviser earned, working exactly the same hours!

And it's not hard to push your career ever-upwards, day-by-day.

The next time you're with a client at the Point of Maximum Excitement (like when they've just had a revelation with you!) simply ask the Golden Referral Question:

"Who's the richest person you know who might benefit from working with me?"

You'll soon be climbing your own wealth ladder alongside the rich and (maybe) famous.

The thing with rules is that they're very black and white.

Binary, if you like.

You either obey a rule, or you break it.

Standards, on the other hand, allow outcomes to be achieved through a variety of actions.

Sometimes rules are useful:

- Do Not Enter: High Voltage
- First across the line wins the race
- Keep Left
- No Naked Flames

Most of the time though, it works better if we set a standard that leads to a desired outcome, rather than prescribing too many rules:

RULE: I must work until I get three clients today
STANDARD: I'm always open to opportunity and will grasp it wherever I see it

RULE: I will never say anything to offend anyone
STANDARD: I will always behave as my authentic self

RULE: I must never eat chocolate
STANDARD: I will eat a balanced diet

RULE: No refunds!
STANDARD: I will deliver value that amazes and delights

The other great thing about standards is that the higher you raise them, the less you need rules at all.

When you're driving a racecar, as I sometimes do, weight is everything. So much so, that most regulations include a minimum weight for all competitors. Stray below it, and you're out.

Of course, you can't afford to be too heavy either. Every extra kilo above the minimum allowed, and you're giving away precious laptime to the leaner opposition. Mechanics will shave layers of paint from a bodyshell to save a few grams.

The team even calculates how much fuel the car will use lights-to-flag, and puts exactly that amount in the tank.

Stuttering to a halt just after you've zoomed victorious past the chequer is the best possible vindication that they got it just right. That also explains why there's a rich history of racecars running out of fuel before the race has finished!

In business too, there's no shame in winning a client, finishing a project or launching a product just in time, and with the minimum of extra weight or padding.

In fact lean, agile and innovative have become bywords for success in the digital age.

Trim out words, paragraphs, costs, people and anything you can to get a winning impact as efficiently as possible.

Don't cut it too fine though.

FREQUENTLY ASKED...

If a coaching support site had an FAM (Frequently Asked Moans) section, this is how it'd probably read:

M: I can't get my Buffer/Tweet Adder/ManyChat to automatically get potential clients contacting me.

A: Neither can anyone else, because that's not the way the world works. Put some time into nurturing relationships, give value, and your clients will begin to announce themselves to you.

M: Nobody wants to buy my course, which I just spent 3 months creating.

A: Maybe you should have spent 3 months instead talking to your ideal clients and getting into their world of pain and desires. Then you could have built something they actually wanted.

M: My mate's a coach, and he's got three houses and two Mercs. Why haven't I?

A: Not all coaches are successful, but some just work harder, smarter and/or get lucky. Stop comparing yourself to others and be the best version of yourself you can be.

M: Why do I keep getting asked for refunds?

A: Probably because you're not listening. Ask everybody who wants their money back, why? Make a list of reasons and engineer them out of your business, one-by-one.

M: Why do I keep getting blocked on Facebook?

A: I'd answer that, but you're blocked so I can't see you.

There's a saying in the transformation business:

The only way to make a lot of money is to help a lot of people.

Of course, in both halves of that statement, some perspective on what constitutes "a lot" is required.

Even so, it's a kind of truism.

Except.

There's a reason why Porsche is the most profitable car company in the world, and it applies to any business, including yours.

What if you could help FEWER people, yet make MORE money?

Only three simple things have to be in place for that to happen:

1. You provide a service that gives a massive transformational impact and value
2. You charge what it's worth to the buyer, not what it costs you to deliver
3. You provide it only to people who can afford it

Whether that helps LOTS of people and makes you LOTS of money is still a matter of perspective, on both counts.

But it's a good start.

Author Chris Brogan writes about the three levers you can pull to accelerate your business growth and revenue:

1. Velocity – does this get the buyer what she wants faster?
2. Friction – does this remove complexity or annoyance for the buyer?
3. Connectedness – is this something worth sharing with others?

Every idea you have starts off with a measure of each of those. Even if it's close to zero, that's still a measure, right?

Think of them like aircraft thrust levers, where the more you pull them, the more noise, excitement and acceleration you get.

How much more can you pull your levers?

If you're wondering why your email content isn't getting read, or getting you any more business, here are 5 ways you can start to turn that around:

- **CONVERSATION** – too many emails are dry, corporate and overly promotional. Write like you're talking to a friend at the mythical water-cooler.

- **HEADLINE** – make the subject Useful, Urgent, Unique and Ultra-specific.

- **SPLIT-TEST** – Send different versions with varied content, headlines, and timing to see which gets a better response.

- **CALL TO ACTION** – If you want a direct result, ask a direct question. What should the reader do after they read your email?

- **GET MORE READERS** – Promote your email subscription whenever you can in social media. New sign-ups are the lifeblood of your business.

Crafting the perfect email campaign is a complex art that you can always learn and improve, but try those for starters.

I read a coach recently saying she felt embarrassed to post client testimonials on her social media in case we all thought she was bragging.

So the question is, should you do this, and how?

Like many other aspects of self-promotion, the answer's in the nuance. Building a tribe of raving fans is a wonderful asset – some might say essential – but there's no need to be braggy about it.

Saying, **"Look! Another client saying how amazing I am!"** is one thing.

Another thing entirely is taking the opportunity to demonstrate social proof and remind potential future clients how they might benefit from working with you:

"I'm so excited that xxxxx got such a great result from our work together. If her experience resonates, let's talk about how we could get the same for you."

That's not bragging, it's just giving us an insight into your world, your power and your value.

Whatever you do in life, it's important to understand the value of what you do to the world, to the market, and to others.

Marketing icon Mike Dillard describes the three factors that dictate how much money you can make:

1. **Competition** – The number of people who are also capable of performing any particular job.

2. **Education** – The amount of specialised skills or training needed to perform the job.

3. **Leverage** – The number of people around the world which your work benefits or impacts on.
4.

Let's look at some examples:

- A global sports champion scores highly in all three, so gets incredibly wealthy

- A brain surgeon scores VERY highly in one and two, but poorly in three, so does well but doesn't become a multi-millionaire

- A waiter scores poorly in all three, so stays relatively poor

Now, let's apply the three-factor test to you, as a coach, therapist or trainer:

- Clearly, if you don't have a unique voice, talent or offering you fail on number 1.

- If your skill-level is poor, that's number 2 knocked over as well.

- Finally, if you stay rooted in old-school, one-on-one, face-to-face training or coaching, your leverage score is lousy too.

Dillard calls the sum of the three factors your Personal Value Level, or PVL.

What can you do to increase your PVL?

HUNTED, NOT HUNTER

Most coaches would agree that our marketing Holy Grail is to get more of our ideal clients to find us, so we don't have to find them.

Being chased, rather than chasing, alters the whole dynamic of the prospect/client relationship with you.

• You have more time to actually coach, instead of marketing (which Jonny Hates, as you may know)
• You can charge more, as you're in demand
• You can choose who you take on, and who you don't

If all those things are desirable, how attainable are they?

Well, if you really want to attain them, it comes down to your doing ONE key thing that will give you the keys to the kingdom:

BECOME A LEADER TO YOUR TRIBE

1. Gain skills, knowledge or abilities that few others have, and which mark you out as different and useful
2. Demonstrate the effect that those skills and abilities have on others
3. With this positive social proof, you'll naturally become more confident
4. Confident people are attractive to others
5. With attraction comes your following, and the thrill of being chased.

So, one step at a time: what marks you out as different and useful?

Work on that, the rest falls into place.

WHAT'S YOUR PROPOSAL?

Whatever you're selling, there'll likely be a proposal involved.

Whether it's a car, a house, dental treatment, a new website, a coaching programme or anything else bought and sold person-to-person, you'll make some kind of proposal to which the prospective buyer then says yes or no.

Note: Yes or No.

That's what we want, isn't it? To rule OUT those who don't want to buy, so we can rule IN those who do.

We all know "maybe" , or "I'll think about it" are just timewasting, polite forms of "get lost".

Here's the one sure-fire way to eliminate that wasted time, once and for all:

BE THERE WHEN THEY'RE MAKING THE DECISION TO BUY, OR NOT.

This means:

- Don't send them a proposal by email or post (what?!) to look at. Like, never, ever do that.

- Instead, arrange a meeting to go through the proposal with them.

- Start the meeting by explaining that you're here to go through the proposal together.

- Make it clear that the outcome of the meeting is a yes, or a no. Either is good. Yes is better.

- The same applies if you're verbalising a proposal by phone or video link. Video where possible, of course.

Did I mention never to send them a proposal to look at?

Oh yeah, I did. Good.

As I sweated, groaned and complained at my personal trainer about the way he was pushing me, he hit me with a smart one-liner. He's quite the philosopher, young Brenton.

He said, Jonny, the way you do anything is the way you do everything.

In other words:

- If you give up here before you're done, you'll give up everywhere before you're done
- If mediocre is your standard here, it's probably your standard whatever you're doing
- If you don't care about your fitness, you don't care about much else either

The ability to push yourself – or find someone else who can push you – in all areas of your life is a critical piece in the success jigsaw.

The next time I'm stuck for words to finish a post, video or email, I'll think of that last agonising press-up, and push on through the pain.

Being a big fish in a small pond must feel kinda cool.

You know, that whole vibe:

- Being admired for your size and stature
- Getting respect and fear from the little fishes
- No worries about anyone picking an argument
- Knowing exactly where all your boundaries are
- You can outpace the other fishes with hardly any effort

On the other hand...

Imagine leaping across the small grassy divide into another, really big pond. Suddenly:

- You feel uncomfortable and intimidated to start with
- But, you see how much more room there is to grow
- There are HUGE, fast fishes who you can swim with
- It hits you how little you really knew back in that grubby lil' puddle
- Soon your new pond feels normal, and you realise you're twice the size you were before!

If you do ONE smart thing different this year, pick a bigger pond.

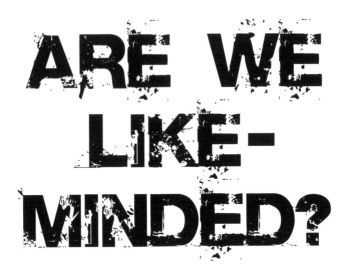

Someone contacted me on LinkedIn recently because they were looking to "connect with people similar to them".

Surely one of the great misunderstandings about networking and relationships in general is that we should strive to hang out with "like-minded individuals".

Firstly, that's fundamentally nonsense, as everyone has their own, unique mind, but even if we take it at face-value it still doesn't make much sense.

What do you think is the most that could happen if you regularly interact with people who are just like you, in the same profession and at the same point in their journey?

1. You chew the fat over how the job/life/the economy sucks for you right now
2. You get validation for all the dumb ideas you imagine might be working
3. You support each other in staying exactly where you are

On the other hand, what might happen if you reached out to people in entirely different walks of life, and maybe even more successful than you?

1. You get access to fresh thinking and ideas
2. You get open critique of what you're doing, and how
3. You get offers of support to make you more successful

That seems like a better way to network, right?

I love that movie so much I bought the full-price Blu-Ray like a sucker, but the 8-foot blue weirdos are nowhere near the most powerful avatar experience I've had.

Not even close.

I love creating my customer avatars even more, and so will you.

Before you hit the airwaves like a manic 80s radio DJ, blasting your wonderful weirdness out to anyone listening, take a breath and write down exactly who you'd like to be working with.

More importantly, who'd like to be working with you.

When I say EXACTLY who, I mean:

- What's their name? (Think of one that suits)
- What do they look like? (Pick a Google image)
- How old are they? (+/- 5)
- What do they want more than anything?
- What are they desperate to get away from?
- How can you help?

When you've got that nailed, you've got a chance of actually finding them, and they you.

THE PERFECT WEBSITE

Of course, there's no such thing, although some are better than others.

Here's a quick checklist to see if you've got the fundamentals of a great coaching website in place:

- Clear call-to-action above the fold – where it can be seen at first view
- No distracting social media icons right at the top
- Attractive imagery that pampers the eye
- Simple benefit statement in the headline – what problem are you solving, or desire serving?
- Less you, more them
- No waffle
- Definitely no typos

You have a problem if we land on your site right now, and we have to spend more than three seconds answering the questions:

- Why am I here?
- What's in it for me?
- What am I supposed to do next?

Clarity and simplicity wins every time.

I had a coach ask recently how he could swing people into his paid coaching, after he'd already "solved all their problems" on the initial introduction call.

Here's how I unpack that one:

- It's irresponsible to "coach" someone you just met, as you can't possibly know enough about who they are or what they want to offer any kind of useful solution.

- An initial call should be about discovering what they need, and calibrating whether you're the right person to provide that.

- The client's unlikely to value what you give her for free, and therefore won't take any action on your advice. That way, you both lose.

- It's inconceivable that you can solve any deep problems, feed any meaningful desires or drive lasting transformation in a single call. Just not possible.

- Finally, why give your best stuff away? Learn to charge what you're worth, and build meaningful relationships of impact and mutual value.

I could go on, but in case you're still unclear:

Don't coach for free.

Have you ever been persuaded to take someone on because your financial brain said yes, even though your heart said no?

As a coach, I sometimes get asked to work with less-than-ideal clients.

Here's the thing: you can totally choose who you work with.

In fact, it's probably the most important choice you will ever make in your coaching practice.

Your ideal clients will:

- Pay you what you're worth
- Make you feel great about working with them
- Benefit the most from what you do to help them
- Work with you for longer, making hustling for new business less critical
- Act as advocates for you and your services

The opposite is almost always true of your only-there-cos-they-pay-you clients.

It's time to get full "Sir Alan" with anyone you're not happy with, and don't worry about the money.

When I recently fired two of my clients, I had two new wonderful, perfect folks join within three days.

Funny how the world works, eh?

I triggered a lively debate on social media the other day about whether a coach also needs to be a salesperson.

Half the comments said no, you should never sell. Just let the customer decide.

The other half were like, sell as hard as you need to make them a customer.

Here's the thing: both approaches are right. It comes down to how you define "selling".

WHAT SELLING ISN'T:

- Hammering away after a customer says no
- Dropping your price to tempt a reluctant buyer
- Serving a 45 minute canned pitch to wear them into submission

WHAT SELLING IS:

- Engaging with an ideal client who'd benefit from what you do
- Presenting them a compelling solution at a price they can afford
- Guiding them to make a decision in their best interest

If you do that regularly, you'll thrive, and so will they.

Nothing "salesy" about that, is there?

Building a modern coaching, training or therapy practice gives you the opportunity to do what would have seemed impossible a few years ago.

It's called time-leverage, and from the outside it looks and feels like you actually MADE more time.

Here are the building-blocks to get you to that point:

- Stop doing non-essential stuff. You already know what that is, don't you?
- Automate everything you can. The tools are easy to find
- Engage trainers and coaches of your own so you don't have to learn from YOUR mistakes
- Delegate whatever needs doing, but doesn't need you doing it
- Create passive income from subscriptions to low/medium priced programmes
- Switch from 1-2-1 sessions to group programmes

The only thing that'll stop any of those things working is if you never get started.

Pick one. Start today.

The death of email has been grossly exaggerated.

In fact, it's more and more the only thing that is actually yours.

By which I mean...

- Your Facebook profile, page or group isn't yours
- Your Instagram account isn't yours
- Your Twitter account isn't yours
- Your LinkedIn contacts aren't yours (although you can download their email addresses – for now)

They belong to the faceless monolithic corporations who run them.

On the other hand, your email list and the stuff you write and send out can't be hijacked, banned or closed down by anybody.

Use social media to its fullest, of course.

But always respect, protect and nurture what's truly yours at the same time.

Remember how we started out talking about the three things you need to do BEFORE you start marketing?

I've been hanging out with transformation professionals for over two decades, and I've noticed how the most successful have put in place those three basic pillars, which support everything else they do.

Here's how you can get started building them too:

1. **WHAT**: Understand your great gift, your ONE thing that you bring to the world. Your WHAT should be a holy alliance of what you CAN do, what you LOVE to do, and what you can get PAID for.

2. **WHO**: Knowing who your ideal clients are is a key foundational understanding, but one which is often missed. You can't serve everyone, so working out who needs it, who wants it and why is absolutely critical.

3. **HOW**: Only when you've nailed down your WHAT and your WHO can you consider building your HOW. This is your product range, your delivery method, your marketing channels, and all the associated tools, tactics and strategies that you use around them.

That s**t is hard, but way harder if you try it before the other two...

How effectively have you built your Three Pillars?

I was eating a banana last night, and reflecting on what a thoughtfully convenient little fruit it really is:

- You can see from the outside if it's to your taste – green, yellow, brown it goes.
- It's so easy to unpack and get to what's inside
- Not messy and you can easily consume it when you're mobile
- Delicious and leaves you feeling satisfied
- Great value for all the benefits it provides

Earlier in the afternoon, I'd wrestled with an orange, that by contrast:

- Was a massive challenge to get into
- Lots of wasted rind and pith to scrape off
- Made my eyes sting as it squirted its evil juices at me
- Was sour as hell inside, and loads of work just to find out
- Gave me next to no reward for all the effort

Can you see where this is going?

That's right.

If you're trying to sell me something, let me put it this way.

Less orange. More banana

When you're speaking, broadcasting or writing, it's always a good idea to be authentic, to be you.

Actually, scratch that.

It's a must.

Let your personality shine through.

Tell your story.

But deeper than that, it's sometimes good to dig into the dark days of your past, to reveal stuff that you're not proud of, or that went wrong all by itself, and certainly wouldn't want to replicate now.

Of course, we don't want to JUST read your sob stories, hard-luck disasters or family tragedies day in, day out.

But, just once in a while, let's see what you've battled through, and won, to become who you are today.

I've become pretty fanatical recently about getting paid EVERY day by somebody.

I don't mean booking something, or invoicing someone.

I mean *PING*-you-just-got-some-money-in-your-bank kind of paid.

You see, once you decide that every day counts, that a day without pay is a day wasted, then you'll naturally do all this good stuff:

- Hang out with your ideal clients every day
- Make at least one offer every day
- Talk to people who want to work with you every day
- Continually ask how you can help
- Hone and refine your work, every day

Money aside, isn't that what you should be doing anyway, every day?

It's easy to casually mix-up the terms strategy and tactics, and it's understandable why.

Both refer to how you show up in the world, but both are different parts of that whole, and both are essential elements of success.

Here are some examples to explain:

Strategy: I use Facebook Groups to attract and engage my ideal clients
Tactics: I invite people I'd like to join. I post 3 times a day. I broadcast regular live shows.

Strategy: I grow an email list to make it easier to communicate directly
Tactics: I have a subscriber capture and incentive on my website. I email something useful and informative every day

Strategy: I only work with people I know I can help
Tactics: I promote my services clearly and without exaggeration. I carefully interview potential clients to make sure we fit.

Strategy is WHAT you do to meet your goals. Tactics are HOW you do it.

Are you doing enough of both?

Today's been a relatively slow day for me.

I had a bunch of brilliant conversations with members in my Group, and a short podcast interview with some crazy Americans.

After a manic day yesterday, I needed to wind down a bit.

And don't ever feel guilty about doing the same. Nobody can operate at full pelt day-after-day.

Anyway, it's impossible to literally do NOTHING – as long as you're breathing, you're doing SOMETHING, right? – and you'll be surprised just how much you get done when you slow to a crawl.

Looking around my desk this evening, I realise I've made copious notes, had at least three brain-dumps, and come up with two really cracking ideas that I'm going to fire into action next week.

And all that because I was too tired to do anything much at all.

You Didn't Think I'd Leave It At 99, Did You?

VALUES – THE BONUS 100th

The Heart And Soul Of Your Business (And Your Life)

If you've read this far, you'll have understood some of the mindset, strategies and tactics which I deploy in my coaching practice.

Aside from all that practical stuff, I often get asked about my values.

As in, "what are your values, Jonny?"

So we're clear, I'm using "values" in this context to mean:

Non-negotiable moral or ethical positions which define thoughts, actions and behaviour.

Here are my Five Core Values, which infuse everything I do.

MY CORE VALUE NUMBER ONE :
I always strive to leave the world better than I found it.

The trouble with statements like this, is that they're easily seen as glib, empty promises.

You might say, well so what? Doesn't everybody try and do that?

Well, no. They don't.

Here are some examples of people/organisations who plainly don't care about the mess, misery and suffering they create:

- Cigarette manufacturers
- Gambling organisations
- Some financial advisers
- Most banks
- Drug dealers
- People smugglers
- Oil companies
- Some politicians
- Payday loan companies
- Gun manufacturers

I could go on, but you get the idea.

Is the primary purpose of what you do to improve the world, even one person at a time?

If it is, you share my first value.

MY CORE VALUE NUMBER TWO:
I'd rather turn away a client than work with the wrong one.

Here are some examples of the "wrong" clients for me:

- They expect a get-rich-quick solution
- They're in it only for the money
- I'm not sure I can help them
- They've had a dozen coaches before and are still failing
- They haggle over the price
- They appear overly needy and demanding
- They want me to Do It For Them
- They want me to find them clients

I could go on, but you get the idea.

My goal is to equip all my clients with the knowledge, skills, strategies and tactics they need to build their thriving practice and their life of abundance, FOR THEMSELVES!

That's way more powerful than doing it for them, and it's my second core value.

MY CORE VALUE NUMBER THREE:
I always show up authentically

In practice, this means:

- Never trying to be someone I'm not
- Only saying what I know to be true
- Admitting if I don't know the answer
- Owning up to my mistakes
- Doing only what makes me happy
- Confronting injustice or unkindness where I find it
- Hanging out with people I like
- Doing the best work I can, always
- Only teaching what I have proven to work

I could go on, but you get the idea.

What does your authentic self look like?

MY CORE VALUE NUMBER FOUR:
I am always open to change and opportunity

In practice, this means:

- Accepting that learning is a lifelong pursuit
- Not being attached to current habits and behaviours
- Reading books written by others smarter than me
- Continually studying new strategies and tactics
- Considering all offers for joint ventures
- Changing my mind in the light of new evidence
- Striving to be the best version of me I can be, eventually
- Not investing emotionally in anything inanimate
- Going all out to engage with an ideal client
- Stopping what doesn't feel right, right away

I could go on, but you get the idea.

Are you open to change, whenever it feels right?

MY CORE VALUE NUMBER FIVE:
I do everything I can to optimise my health and longevity

In practice, this means:

- Sleeping 8 hours a night
- Regular meditation and conscious breathing
- Eating fresh, raw and plant-based foods whenever possible
- Strength and muscle-conditioning twice a week
- Cardio exercise every day
- Drinking loads of filtered water every day
- Never smoking (duh!) and drinking only a little alcohol
- Regular medical check-ups
- Laughing every day with friends
- Doing only that which makes me happy and content

I could go on, but you get the idea.

What are you doing to keep your mind and body in peak shape?

THE BIG QUESTION

In this last chapter – The Bonus 100th - I've shared my heart and soul with you, and disclosed the five core values which infuse everything I do.

I thought it would be a great way for you to get to know me better, but also to guide you to thinking about your own values.

Why does this matter?

Defining your values is a really important, foundational exercise which you should undertake before you embark on creating a business.

Your values form a kind of immutable template that lays down:

- What you're prepared to do
- What you're not prepared to do
- What you simply can't do
- What you simply can't NOT do
- How you show up to the world

SO: What are your core values?

Drop me an email to jonny@jonnyhates.marketing.

It will get read personally, by me, and I will respond.

EPILOGUE

Thanks for reading...it means a lot that you got this far!

I put Jonny Hates Marketing together to give you a glimpse of the mindset, strategies and tactics I use every day to grow and sustain a thriving coaching business.

In truth, you can apply much of what's in here to pretty much any business, or even if you haven't started one yet!

My mission is to impact on the lives and businesses of 100,000 Change Professionals by 2025. That's 100k coaches, trainers, therapists, consultants and heart-centered entrepreneurs over the next 7 years, as I write this.

History will call me either a visionary or a hopeless dreamer (at best!) on that mission, so here's a couple of ways you can help me to help you on our amazing journeys:

1. Subscribe at www.jonnyhatesmarketing.com. You'll get a FREE Effortless Marketing Blueprint, and instant access to the legendary Daily Brain Tattoos, little sips of Effortless Marketing juice squirted straight into your inbox 6 times a week. (Yes, I know. Not strictly "Daily", but hell, even Jonny takes Sundays off.)

2. Join the Facebook Group after which this book was named. That way you can hang out with me. And a few thousand other interesting folks too.

3. Last, but not least...write a book review on Amazon! Nice if you liked it, but if you didn't, be constructive and tell me why not! I'll make the next one even better, I promise.

Hover your cameraphone over these QR codes to go straight to the goodies!

FREE Three Pillars of Effortless
Marketing Blueprint Download

Join the FREE Jonny Hates
Marketing Facebook Group

RESOURCES

If you like what's in this book and want to read more, then sign up for The Daily Brain Tattoos at
www.jonnyhatesmarketing.com/daily-brain-tattoos

SOME OF MY FAVOURITES

The Prosperous Coach by Steve Chander and Rich Litvin
1001 Ways to Get More Customers by Jonathan Jay
Expert Secrets by Russell Brunson
The Seven Habits of Highly Effective People by Stephen Covey
The Game Changers by Paul Chapman and Julia Roberts
Eat That Frog by Brian Tracy
The 4 Hour Work Week by Tim Ferris
The One Thing by Gary Keller
Build Your Business in 90 Minutes a Day by Nigel Botterill

ABOUT THE AUTHOR

Jonny Hates Marketing and doesn't believe anyone who says they love it.

Jonny Cooper has been helping businesses and their owners make more money, more easily since the turn of the century when he sold his own self-built 8-figure empire and became a full-time coach.

Now he works exclusively with other transformation professionals - coaches, therapists, trainers and consultants – who are looking to build their own life of abundance through a thriving practice.

As a younger man, he got smooth-talked into buying a magic "system" that would **"guarantee a 7-figure launch in 30 days"**.

Mistakenly believing this to mean he would be given a multi-million dollar boat at the end of the month, Jonny was aghast when nothing happened apart from the not-insubstantial transfer of his wealth to the other person, and he developed a scathing abhorrence for sleazy marketers and their lunatic promises.

To this day, he's made it his mission to offer extraordinary value, simplify everything and avoid anything that smacks of hardcore selling.

Jonny truly understands how to position himself and his offering in front of his ideal clients, so they come to HIM instead of him chasing THEM.

Now for the first time, Jonny has compiled 99 of his most powerful hacks, tips and strategies into one concise manual.

Jonny Hates Marketing - Here's how he gets clients diving into his pool without spending a penny on advertising, working like a dog or losing his mind, and how you can too.